WARD KIMBALL

*

ART AFTERPIECES

WITH A FOREWORD BY
Walt Kelly

AN ESSANDESS SPECIAL EDITION
New York

*

It is correct, we believe, to claim that Mr. Kimball's addenda, as they are collected in this volume, are original. The Parisian school of underground poster art says flatly, "Vive le moustache!" This group, claiming to be unique, has in fact produced nothing more than the additives of the mustache, the scrawl of eyeglasses, an occasional monocle (inevitably lopsided), and, if the viewer is lucky, he is treated to a blacked-out tooth in a creamy smile.

Then there are the hackneyed efforts of the imitative American alteration group, the so-called Subway Atelier in New York City. True, these monsters have made use of the added four-letter word across the faces of some of their subjects, but this is merely potential juvenile delinquency and to be classed with the accidental banjo-work of a messy monkey armed with a melting chocolate bar.

Now from the west rises a Lochinvar who is apparently a distinct cut above the messy monkey. In a talk with him this critic learned that Mr. Kimball, a youth of fifty, was disturbed about the publisher's estimate that his work was "unfailingly funny." According to Mr. Kimball, if his work is funny, it has failed. "Cheen Crimes!" exclaimed Mr. Kimball, his mouth full of melted chocolate bar, "this stuff is a lot deeper than they realize. It gets me right about here," he added, putting his hand to his throat.

For the fact of the matter is that Mr. Kimball is a master finisher. He finishes what others have started. Any bull can charge into a china shop, but the bull in this book ENDS the job.

Walt Kelly

PORTRAIT OF NICCOLO SPINELLI

HANS MEMLING

1430? · 1495

VIRGIN AND CHILD

ROGIER VAN DER WEYDEN

1399? · 1464

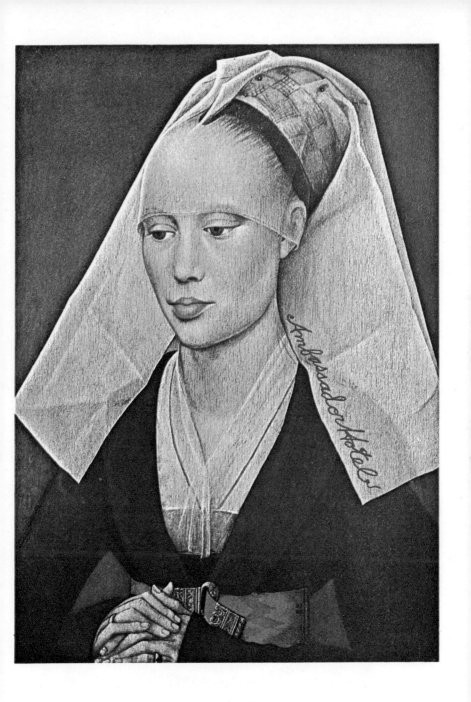

PORTRAIT OF A LADY

ROGIER VAN DER WEYDEN

1399? · 1464

THE GARDEN OF WORLDLY DELIGHTS

HIERONYMUS BOSCH

1450? · 1516

THE MONEYLENDER AND HIS WIFE

QUENTIN MASSYS

1466? · 1530

CARDINAL ALBRECHT AS ST. JEROME

LUCAS CRANACH THE ELDER

1472 · 1553

ST. LUKE DRAWING THE VIRGIN MARY

JAN GOSSAERT

1478? · ?1533

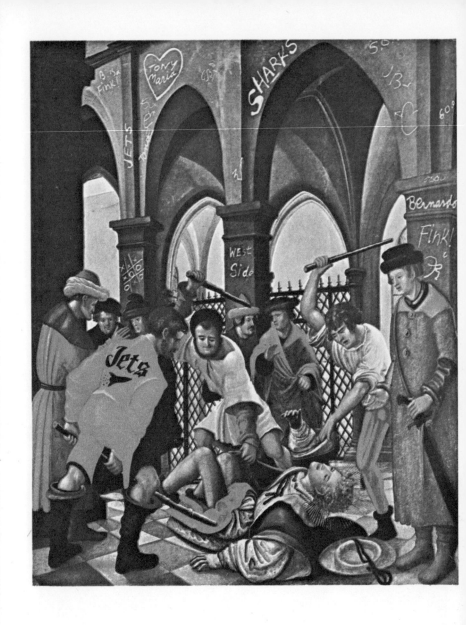

MARTYRDOM OF ST. FLORIAN

ALBRECHT ALTDORFER

1480? · 1538

MONA LISA

LEONARDO DA VINCI

1452 · 1519

EXPULSION FROM PARADISE

GIOVANNI DI PAOLO

1403? · 1482

SAINT APOLLONIA

PIERO DELLA FRANCESCA

1420? · 1492

RENAISSANCE NOBLEMAN

COSIMO TURA

1430? · 1495

THE VISITATION

MARIOTTO ALBERTINELLI

1474 · 1515

THE BIRTH OF VENUS

SANDRO BOTTICELLI

CREATION OF ADAM

MICHELANGELO

1475 · 1564

VENUS AND ADONIS

TITIAN

1477 · 1576

PORTRAIT OF A MAN WITH A MEDAL

SANDRO BOTTICELLI

1444? · 1510

PORTRAIT OF THE DOGE LOREDANO

GIOVANNI BELLINI

1430? · 1516

ALLEGORY

(Alfonso d'Este and Laura Diante)

TITIAN

1477 · 1576

THE CHASTISEMENT OF LOVE

SCHOOL OF CARAVAGGIO

FRANCIS I, KING OF FRANCE

JEAN CLOUET

1485? · 1545

THE ABDUCTION OF
THE DAUGHTERS OF LEUCIPPUS

PETER PAUL RUBENS

1577 · 1640

HELENE FOURMENT

PETER PAUL RUBENS

1577 · 1640

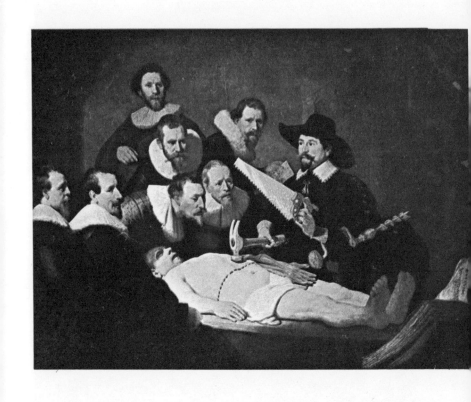

THE ANATOMY LESSON
or
THE ANATOMY OF DR. TULP

REMBRANDT

1606 · 1669

OLD WOMAN CUTTING HER NAILS

REMBRANDT

1606 · 1669

THE ABDUCTION OF THE SABINE WOMEN

NICOLAS POUSSIN

1594 · 1665

ST. JEROME

GIUSEPPE DE RIBERA

1588 · 1652

PORTRAIT OF ARNAULD D'ANDILLY

PHILIPPE DE CHAMPAIGNE

1602 · 1674

COUNT DUKE OF OLIVARES

DIEGO VELÁZQUEZ

1599 · 1660

THE AVENUE

MEINDERT HOBBEMA

1638 · 1709

THE ARTIST IN HIS STUDIO

JAN VERMEER

1632 · 1675

APELLES PAINTING A PORTRAIT OF CAMPASPE

GIOVANNI TIEPOLO

1696 · 1770

A SEAPORT AND CLASSIC RUINS IN ITALY

FRANCESCO GUARDI

1712 · 1793

LE MEZZETIN

JEAN ANTOINE WATTEAU

1684 · 1721

PORTRAIT OF LOUIS XIV

HYACINTHE RIGAUD

1649 · 1743

DIANA

FRANÇOIS BOUCHER

1703 · 1770

MISS WILLOUGHBY

GEORGE ROMNEY

1734 · 1802

WRECK OF THE HOPE

KASPAR DAVID FRIEDRICH

1774 · 1840

MADAME HAMELIN

JACQUES LOUIS DAVID

1748 · 1825

MOUNTED OFFICER OF THE IMPERIAL GUARD

THÉODORE GÉRICAULT

1791 · 1824

THE BLUE BOY

THOMAS GAINSBOROUGH

1727 · 1788

THE SHADY GROVE

JEAN HONORÉ FRAGONARD

1732 · 1806

PINKIE

SIR THOMAS LAWRENCE

1769 · 1830

THE DUCHESS OF ALBA

FRANCISCO DE GOYA

1746 · 1828

GEORGE WASHINGTON

GILBERT STUART

1755 · 1828

THE OLD BRIDGE

HUBERT ROBERT

1733 · 1808

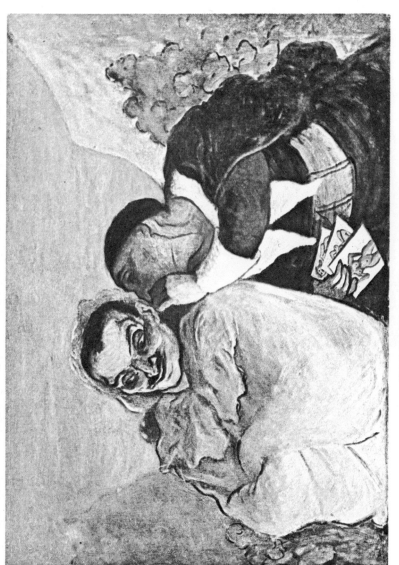

CRISPIN AND SCAPIN

HONORÉ DAUMIER

1808 · 1879

THE GLEANERS

JEAN FRANÇOIS MILLET

1814 · 1875

LUNCHEON ON THE GRASS

ÉDOUARD MANET

1832 · 1883

IN THE BOAT

ÉDOUARD MANET

1832 · 1883

THE FAMILY REUNION

FRÉDÉRIC BAZILLE

1841 · 1870

FUR TRADERS ON THE MISSOURI

GEORGE CALEB BINGHAM

1811 · 1879

AFTER THE HUNT

WILLIAM M. HARNETT

1848 · 1892

THE DRAWBRIDGE

VINCENT VAN GOGH

1853 · 1890

SUNFLOWERS IN A VASE

VINCENT VAN GOGH

1853 · 1890

STILL LIFE

PAUL GAUGUIN

1848 · 1903

NUDE FIXING HER HAIR

EDGAR DEGAS

1834 · 1917

THE FIGHT FOR THE WATER HOLE

FREDERIC REMINGTON

1861 · 1909

THE WHITE GIRL

JAMES MC NEILL WHISTLER

1834 · 1903